State of Vermont
Department of Libraries
Midstate Regional Library
RFD #4
Montpelier, Vt. 05602

King Nimrod's Tower

Text copyright © 1982 by Leon Garfield
Illustrations copyright © 1982 by Michael Bragg
First published in Great Britain in
1982 by Methuen Children's Books Ltd.

All rights reserved. No part of this book may be reproduced or utilized in any form or by any means, electronic or mechanical, including photocopying, recording or by any information storage and retrieval system, without permission in writing from the Publisher. Inquiries should be addressed to Lothrop, Lee & Shepard Books, a division of William Morrow & Company, Inc., 105 Madison Ave., New York, N.Y. 10016.
Printed in Great Britain.

First U.S. Edition
1 2 3 4 5 6 7 8 9 10

Library of Congress Catalog Card Number 81-86470

ISBN 0-688-01288-4
ISBN 0-688-01290-6 (lib. bdg.)

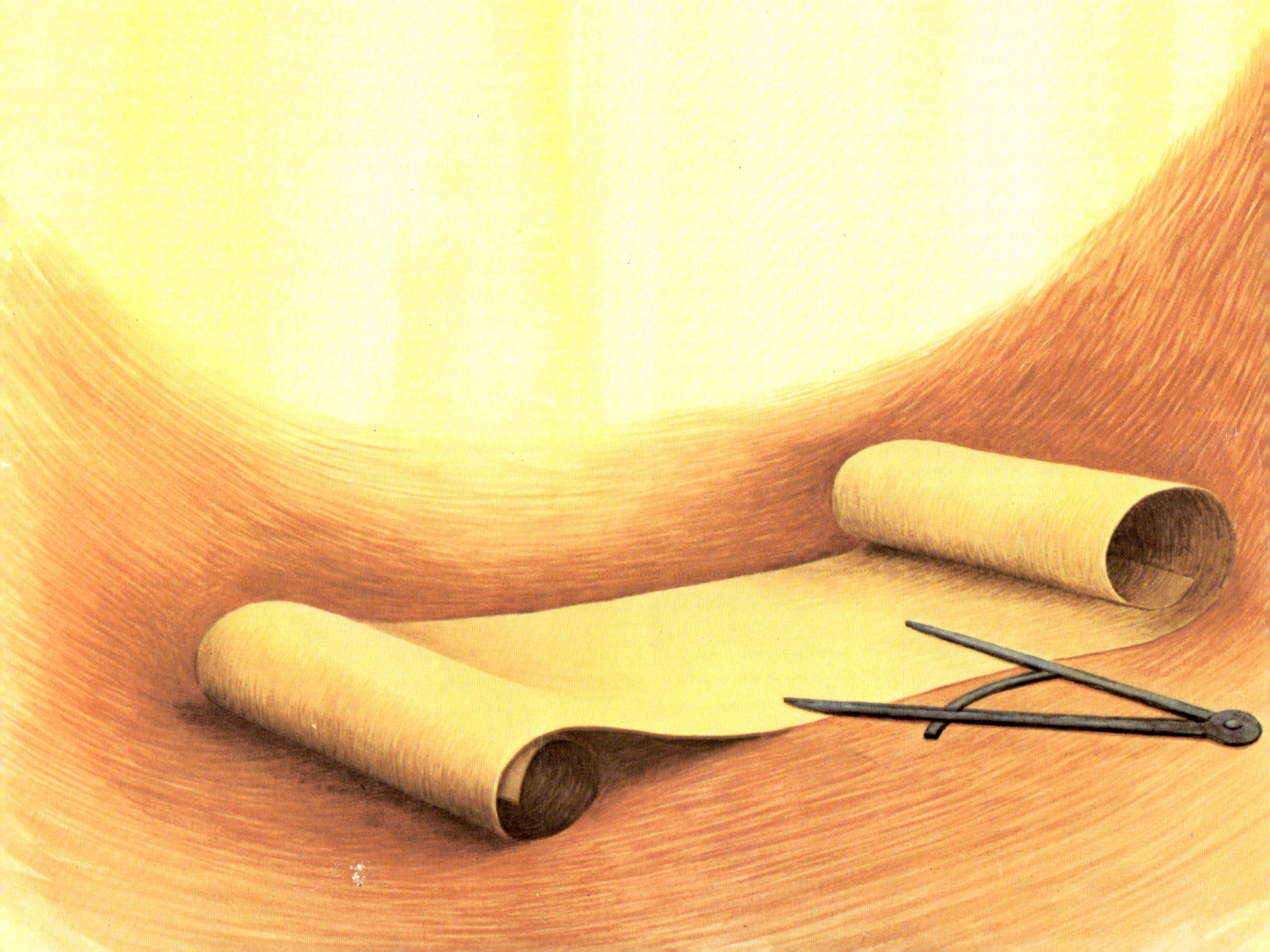

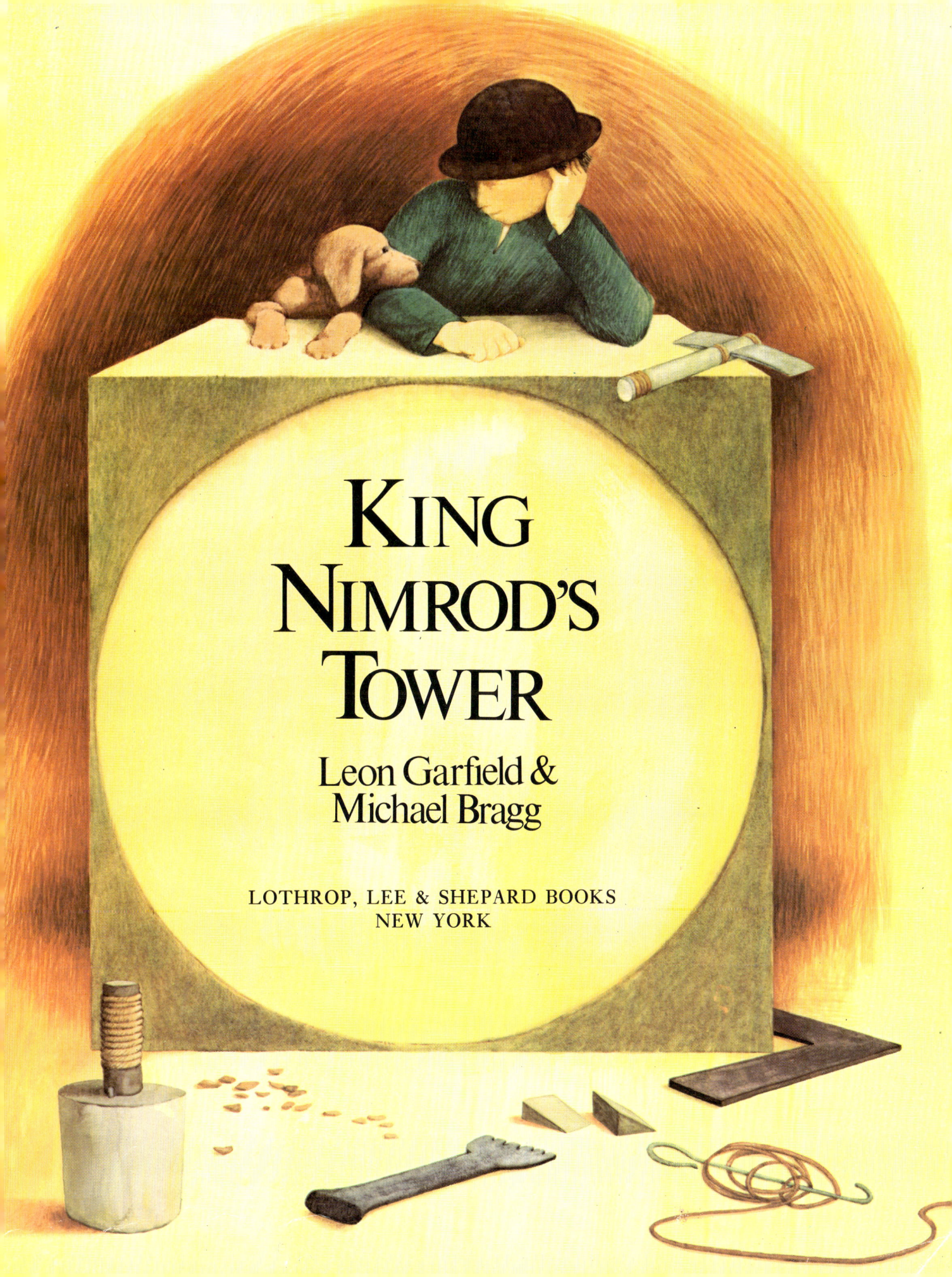

King Nimrod's Tower

Leon Garfield & Michael Bragg

LOTHROP, LEE & SHEPARD BOOKS
NEW YORK

There was a boy in Babylon who found a dog. It was a jumping, whooping, whirling, biting baby of a dog; and it had no friends. The boy called it "Snap", because it snapped; and the dog called him "Wuf!" because that was all it could say.

"I'll take you home with me," said the boy, "if you learn how to behave."

The dog bit his shoe; and whooped like anything.

"But I'll leave you here in the fields if you don't learn to behave."

The dog bit his trousers; and whooped again.

And all the brickmakers, carpenters, stone-workers, architects and surveyors who were working in the fields, laughed till they were told to stop laughing and get on with their work.

King Nimrod was building a tower. It was to be as high as heaven. The spot had been chosen, the stone fetched, the clay dug and the bricks baked. Ten thousand workmen fetched and carried, fetched and carried, and did as they were told.

"Look!" said the boy to the dog. "And try to learn something."

"Hurry!" shouted the foremen. "Hurry along there!"

And the workmen hurried along.

"Lift!" shouted the foremen. "All together now – lift!"

And the workmen lifted.

"Sit!" shouted the boy to the dog. "Sit down, sir!"

The dog bit his sleeve and tore it; and whooped and whirled away.

It was a stupid dog. Its head was as thick as porridge, and its feet were like plates of mud. It would never learn to behave.

"King Nimrod will be walking into heaven," said the boy, "before I can take you back to Babylon, to sleep beside my bed."

King Nimrod's tower was growing fast. With ropes and hoists and cranes and ladders, it rose on a sweep of pillars and stairs. It was a mile round at the bottom, and already it was half an hour high. King Nimrod came to see it; and the ten thousand workmen stood to attention, one upon each of ten thousand steps. He climbed to the top and looked up at the sky, where heaven was waiting behind the clouds.

"God save King Nimrod!" everyone shouted together; and threw up their hats and handkerchiefs and dinner-bundles, till the tower looked like a tree with blossoms tossed up in the wind. "God save the King!"

King Nimrod shook his head and smiled. Soon he would be as high as heaven, and on a level with God.

"King Nimrod will save God," he said. "If God learns to behave."

There was a crack of lightning and a rumble of thunder; and the King said: "See! God is frightened. He is shaking in His shoes!"

"Bow down!" shouted the foremen. "Bow down to King Nimrod the Great!"

And all ten thousand workmen bowed down as low as dust.

"Down!" shouted the boy to the dog. "Down, sir, down!"

The dog bit his shirt and pranced and danced away.

"King Nimrod will be having supper with the angels," said the boy, "before I can take you back to Babylon, to sleep beside my bed."

Higher and higher rose the tower, till the workmen toiled in the clouds. Eagles stole their sandwiches, and rainbows painted their shirts.

"Stay at work!" shouted the foremen. "Stay at work or King Nimrod will stop your pay!"

And the ten thousand stayed hard at work; with bricks and mortar and heavy stones.

"Stay!" shouted the boy to the dog. "Stay or I'll stop your dinner!"

The dog jumped up and tore his collar; and whooped and whirled away.

"King Nimrod will be wearing God's dressing-gown and slippers," said the boy, "before I can take you back to Babylon, to sleep beside my bed."

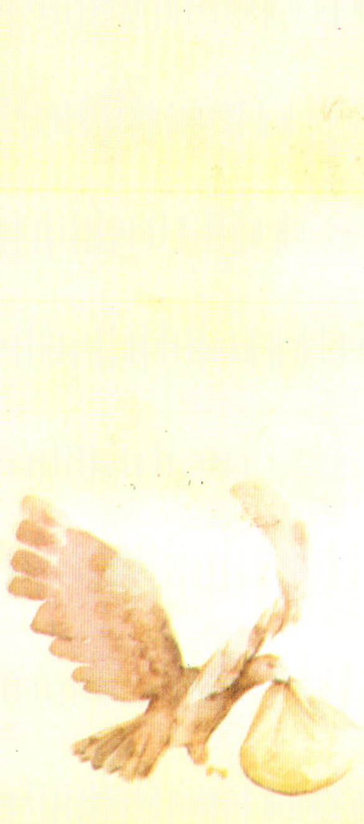

And that was exactly what the angels said to God, who was watching the boy and the dog and not minding King Nimrod in the least.

"My slippers? My dressing-gown?" said God. "That cannot be."

"Behold, O Lord!" said the angels. "The tower is rising fast. Strike it down while there is still time!"

"But if it falls," said God, "the boy and the dog will be sure to perish under all those bricks and stones."

"Then what is to be done?" asked the angels. "How else is King Nimrod to be kept in his place?"

"How many miles to Babylon?" asked God.

"Three score miles and ten."

"Can I get there by candlelight?" asked God.

"Yes, and back again!"

So the angels lighted a candle and God went down into the fields of Babylon, where the foremen shouted and the workmen jumped and obeyed.

"Heave!"
And they all heaved.
"Lift!"
And they all lifted.
"Pull!"
And they all pulled.

Then God smiled and crossed His fingers on every tongue.
"Heave!" shouted the foremen.
And they all lifted.
"Pull!" shouted the foremen.
And they all pushed.
"Lift!" shouted the foremen.
Some pushed, some heaved, and some just sat and scratched their heads.

"What is happening?" shouted the foremen.
"The tower will never get built!"

The workmen stared.

"What was that he said?"

"It sounded like, I must get a haircut!"

"No — no! It was, will you come to dinner tonight?"

"Never! He said his mother had a new dress!"

"Nonsense! He said, my feet are killing me!"

"You must be deaf! I heard it plain as anything. He said, is it time to go home yet?"

In the twinkling of an eye, and without a single lesson, they were all talking in languages they had never talked before! In Swedish, German, Spanish, Hebrew, Greek, Latin and Japanese... though to each and every one, it sounded like plain double-Dutch!

In vain the foremen shouted; in vain King Nimrod raged! The workmen heaved bricks where they should have put statues, and dug holes where they should have built stairs. In vain the foremen threatened; in vain King Nimrod stormed.

Nobody could understand them any more. And worse! The workmen couldn't understand each other, so they just downed tools and left. They left the tower, they left the fields of Babylon, and wandered far and wide. Soon the great tower stood alone, crusted all over with pillars and piped with stairs, like an unfinished pie in the sky.

King Nimrod walked in the fields, as miserable as sin.

"My tower!" he wept. "My beautiful tower that was to have reached heaven! Alas! No more!" But he could not even understand himself; and he drifted away like the dust. The boy and the dog were left all alone.

"Sit!" said the boy to his dog. "I only want to be your friend."
And the dog sat.

"Stand up!" said the boy to his dog. "I only want to take you home."
And the dog stood up.

"Good!" said the boy. "Now I can take you back to Babylon, and you can sleep beside my bed!"

So they went.

"How did it happen?" marvelled the angels. "At last!"

"Because My Kingdom of Heaven is better reached," said God, "by a bridge than by a tower."

P MRL
Garfield, Leon
　King Nimrod's tower

OCT. 19 1995
RSX 10/96
　28
RSX 3/00
RSX 3/01

DATE DUE